Also by Laura Passin

Borrowing Your Body
All Sex and No Story (chapbook)

WE THE DESTROYERS

Laura Passin

Riot in Your Throat
publishing fierce, feminist poetry

Passin, Laura.
1st edition.
ISBN: 979-8-9889898-8-2

Cover Art: Gwendal Cottin (unsplash.com)
Cover Design: Kirsten Birst
Book Design: Shanna Compton
Author Photo: Laura Passin

Riot in Your Throat
Arlington, VA
www.riotinyourthroat.com

for Laura Paul Watson (1980–2024)

"It happens / now. It has already happened. No one is coming."

—Claire Wahmanholm,
"Poem That Cries Wolf"

"Every artist is a cannibal
Every poet is a thief
All kill their inspiration
And sing about the grief"

—U2, "The Fly"

CONTENTS

III: UNMENDED

IV: LOVING THE FIRE

V: POEMS FROM HAVEN

VI: WE RUIN EVERYTHING

I. COWARDLY GODS

GRIEF COUNSELING IN THE LATE ANTHROPOCENE

When the world ends, it will not
matter who, exactly, left it early—

the years shaved off the living
heart, the brain cells torqued

and plaqued by damaged genes.
It will not matter

that once the Cuyahoga lit up
like a factory dying, that the water bequeathed

to the Great Lakes by tired glaciers corroded
ships and fish alike. What we leave behind

is massive, minute: a layer of unusual soil
that circles a moment,

a diseased ring in the globe's bark.
That's how we figured out

what ate the dinosaurs:
a strange signature, everywhere.

No one will miss us.
We are the comet ourselves.

TELL ME, WHAT ELSE SHOULD I HAVE DONE?

after Mary Oliver

I left home. I did not go back.
I didn't drive a car
for 25 years, I took the train,
the bus, I walked
until my heels bled.
I taught *Huck Finn* to adults
and Adrienne Rich to children.
I dropped morphine
into my mother's
starving mouth.
I marched against the war
and then the other war
and then the secret civil war.
I quit dieting.
I told men they were wrong.
I wore my mask.

Prayer is nothing.

I paid attention, but
to what, to what?
The city still erodes,
the lake still eats the shore.
The trees are still burning,
the animals shrieking inside.
My brother's bones
still break and break.

Who made the world?

This world, I mean,
the one gone to seed in our hands.

ON LAKE ERIE WITH MY BROTHER'S GHOST

after Joannie Stangeland

In this boat, we each have an oar.
I am rowing forward, horizon-minded.
He rows differently: at first I think
he is against me, rowing into the past,
aiming for return. He is stronger,
longer arms, so the boat begins to spin.
But we are not going backwards after all;
he sweeps his hand, shows me the whole
snow-swept lake. He wants me to remember
that once, we shared a shore.

SELF-TRIPTYCH

1.

I believe in God the way I believe in ASMR:
something pleasant that happens to other people.
I still can't sleep at night.

2.

I come from a long line of believers, married to—
and divorced from—a long line of unbelievers.
I fall to my knees only when my ankle gives out.

3.

My brain longs for wonder but lives in doubt.
Of my parents, named for saints, the lone survivor
is Thomas: his hand unflinching, not yet finding the wound.

COLD ABECEDARIAN ENDING WITH A LINE
FROM EMILY DICKINSON

Apocalypse cold.
Barbarous cold. What lies beneath
cold. Bites your eyes cold.
Don't breathe cold.
Ear piercing cold.
Fuck you cold.
God is dead cold. God is
here cold.
If only you knew cold. Moons of
Jupiter cold.
Knees on fire cold.
Lighthouse fallen cold.
Miami iguanas falling from trees cold.
Nobody notices you're missing cold.
Old boyfriend never loved you cold.
Permafrost cold.
Quicksilver-solid cold.
Red cold. Lake
Superior
tsunami cold.
Underworld cold.
Very fucking cold cold.
Water freezes to your tear ducts cold.
X-ray reveals cold.
Your surgery is canceled due to cold.
Zero at the bone cold.

"ARCTIC HEAT RECORD IS LIKE MEDITERRANEAN, SAYS UN"

Truth is like beauty,
     says Keats

               TV is like shame,
                   says Anne Carson

A blackbird is like another blackbird,
     says Stevens

               A blackbird is like the same blackbird,
                   says Stevens

The present is like the past,
     says my history professor

               The present is like the future,
                   says my mother's ghost

TOM AND JASPER

My father says, casually,
he's not sure who

will live longer, him
or the dog. One is 12.

One is 78. Not a working hip
between them, though only one

has replaced gnawed-up bone
with titanium ball and plastic socket.

One wandered, rootless,
on the dirt roads

of New Mexico.
One retired.

One lost his way.
One lost his wife.

One understands Spanish,
one a little Japanese.

After the worst thing happened,
one let me cry on his neck

for hours, all salted and cracked.
One saw me safely home.

One is an irreplaceable assortment
of atoms, untraceable electrical arcs,

a universe inside the universe,
a self that will never be repeated,

come the terrible seas
to swallow us all.

And so is the other.

FOR MARY ANN, FIFTEEN YEARS TOO LATE

I thought
    after the funeral

that I would
    take the needles

and complete
    the nearly-knit

peach cotton scarf
    as tribute

to your life—
    just seed

stitch, after all,
    I could do that,

just knit purl knit
    purl and stagger

the pattern to create
    the texture

like a row of sown
    seeds—but

you had thirty years
    on me

to practice the craft,
       such steady

and precise work,
       better hands;

I could not make
       myself

ruin the last piece
       you touched,

let my clumsy
       young grief

graft an elegy
       to what had ended already—

SOLSTICE OR SOMETHING

My friends the pagan farmers
use no electric light from December 1st
until solstice—they honor darkness,
its deepening hold. They know how
to butcher an animal, even one
with a name, because it has served
its purpose on earth. I tell them
that when it all goes to hell,
I'm making my way to them
to ride out the end of days.

I can be useful
with more than words:
I can knit, I can keep
small things warm.

*

If you could move as fast as light,
time would stand still
around you.

*

Every year I am supposed to believe
that something comes back,
that December is a dark womb
from which we are all reborn.
That is what Jesus is,
what Persephone is.
Every day, a nuzzle of light.

I don't buy it.

When something dies
and comes back
we mostly call that
a monster.

*

This year, it didn't snow all autumn
so we have to water the wintering plants.
Otherwise they will really die underneath
while they seem to die above.

*

This time last year my cat was dying,
and this time the year before that
my other cat was dying,
and now I think my dog
is probably dying
when I have the courage
to look death straight
in its toothless little face.

*

This burning planet:
Oh, we have killed you.

It's only fair you take us too.

SELF-PORTRAIT AS COWARDLY GOD

The old dog shakes and squirms as I place her on the chair
where she spends her days, these days.

She can barely see, barely hear, but still
each morning she seems to love her life,

all wiggles and shimmies, that irresistible tail,
so I clothe my fear,

name myself merciful,
let her live.

IF YOU WANT PEACE, PREPARE FOR WAR

The chimp army grins
as its footmen tear
the rival infant limb
from limb. Sir

David Attenborough
insists we cannot know
what motivates
these almost-men.

I beg the camera,
turn away, as one soldier
starts to gnaw the foot
his comrade offers.

The lens does not obey.
The films they make
about the human animal
will be unkind.

*

By the time the Others
find our world, no one
has survived it.
They reconstruct us

from our garbage,
glue fossils in agonized
postures, give names
to the nations we burned.

They put a placard
by the bones
of a sea-blue songbird,
describing the cage.

WING-DEEP IN GIN AND TONIC

Where I'd be if I were an angel

                or a statue of an angel

or a bird

                or an idea of a bird

Drown me in something that is not the burning ocean

                or the fuel-soaked lake

If we can't save this planet

                how drunk do we have to get

                to find another

If we pile into generation ships

who among us will be called Noah

                everywhere Atlantis

                nowhere Ararat

When the monks who "saved civilization"

                illuminated their Bibles

they first killed a calf

                and scraped all trace of life

from its tanned hide

                a book made of dead things

all books are

        dead things

        and soon the Earth

its own abandoned

        archive

II: YOU ARE THE ELEGY YOURSELF

INHERITANCE

The family tree
        in an alphabet
                I can't read

because my great-
        grandfather lived
                to lose his god

and I was given
        to another. A palimpsest
                of dangerous genes.

An eyeblink of a memory
        of snow, the lake,
                the star-strewn lake,

oh, the lake in the snow.

YOU, MEG MURRY

Look at me and all these metaphors:
predictable, annoying

in my starry wonder, my Armageddon
fears, my space-flung mother.

Read *A Wrinkle in Time*
once too often as a girl

and you are there forever,
trapped on an Earth

you so badly—so sincerely—
want to tesser away.

Let's say it's all true.
Let's say there's a way

to fold time and space
that I am almost seeing

in my periphery, on the verge
every time I write.

Where is it, exactly,
I want to go?

To that hideous plaid couch,
the morning news whispering

in the kitchen, the lamp haloing
the book in my hands, my mother

the very age I am now,
walking in with her murky Folger's,

not knowing how cruelly
I want to escape. Look at her

and all these memories:
I think if I fold the paper right,

she might be alive inside it.

MOTHER / DAUGHTER

Your ghost is now thirteen,
an impish girl, rolling

her eyes at me, humiliated
by my existence,

my insistence that she stay
in sight, that she's only

a child (it's dangerous
out there), that she never

leave me.

YOUNGEST CHILD TRIOLET

Brother, brother, sister, brother, brother:
I entered the world already surrounded.
(They tell me I look just like my ~~mother~~.)
Brother, brother, sister, brother, brother—
we all die for one reason or another.
I was desperate for quiet, hated when I found it.
Brother, brother, sister, brother, ~~brother~~:
I'll enter the next world already surrounded.

WATER / POLLUTION

The octopus is not the ink:
      the ink is the hole
            where the octopus was.

*

Whole reefs of coral burn
      acid-white, memorials
            to their own bodies.

*

The stenciled fish
      by the sewer grate where trash
            runs straight to the river.

*

The Kodachrome sunsets over Lake Erie,
      those motes of industrial waste shimmering
            like the world ending.

*

My brother's ashes swirling white by the shore,
      blowing, blown. Water: dust:
            dust.

EKPHRASIS ON AN OUT-OF-FOCUS PHOTO SCANNED BY MY AUNT

My brother plays cello,
        staring at the sheet music I hold
                for him in my little hands—

before I started playing violin,
        before we owned music stands
                and the house was filled

with noise, basement to attic.
        We are both so young,
                neither of us wears glasses—

which means I don't remember this,
        I was so small
                and the world was so blurry.

I walked around knowing nothing,
        storing nothing. No one
                noticed because look

how *helpful* I was, *a good girl,*
        my body like a part of the house
                itself. Reliable. Quiet.

Then they realized I couldn't see,
        not really, and with the glasses came
                my appetite for the world,

sprung from me fully formed.
        I held my own with all
                those boys—yelling, singing,

eating, running. I grew tall.
   My brother grew taller.
      I grew loud.

My brother grew quiet.
   I don't know when he stopped
      playing,

but he did, long before
   I put down my violin.
      And he died, just now,

just this year, because when the pain came
   he did not yell, he did not ask
      for help, he took it and he took it.

I want to show him how it was
   when he was small and loud,
      when he made music

I held in the air for him,
   when he sang to a world
      I could not even see.

IT'S BEETHOVEN'S (D. 1827) BIRTHDAY

which means it's my grandfather's (d. 2003)
birthday,

all the NPR announcers
conspiring

to send me back thirty, no, thirty-five?
Decembers,

playing "Happy Birthday"
terribly

in the kitchen, plastic handset of the
landline

held aloft by my mother
(d. 2009)

my chin squared firmly on my rented
violin.

Keep practicing and I'll buy you your own,
he said

     and he did.

TO OUTWEIGH

*"For every person in the world, more than their body weight
in stuff is now being produced each week."*

—from the BBC News article "Human-made objects
to outweigh living things," December 9, 2020

In the hoarded-out basement
of my parents' house, the strata
of my siblings' heavy nothings
waits to be exhumed,
an archaeology of American failure
to know what is worth
keeping.

Look there, under the box
mislabeled KITCHEN,
an asphalt-black case:
my childhood violin.
Wood warped and split,
bow crushed under
junkweight.

Once I was made
of music, a singing thing.

Now the news says
my doppelgänger of garbage
stillbirths herself each week

as I try to make myself
want less, miss less,
take up less space.

ESCAPING / AIR

rich men riding rockets
    just to say they could

one billion lungs
    keeping watch

dollars made garbage
    dust to dust

a volcano unravels
    punches the stratosphere

with ash
    seen from space

something underneath us
    does not want us

on its skin
    every shore a tsunami

begging to be born

ELEGY WITH CULTURE SHOCK

Oh sunburnt knees and lime-sweet water,
    Carolina that tried to kill me
        for not knowing

where I was not
    wanted: You hold my mother's ash
        in your red clay mouth.

DEMENTIA / ELSEWHERE

1.

James Bond walked out
      of the 27″ screen

into our dingy
      living room

took my mother's hand
      dressed her in sequins

skied away
      from the exploding chalet :

When the wind whipped their faces
      I saw her hair fly back

2.

Lake Erie unpolluted itself, turned blue and nearly solid with trout, and my
mother, light as a girl, walked on the shallow ice with no fear, no wheelchair,
walked all the way to Canada, where her father stood on water and told her,
Don't bother having kids, and she wrote a novel about a brilliant woman with
a tyrannical father and six children and early-onset Alzheimer's and the film
of it won Julianne Moore an Oscar in a divine green gown.

3.

Well of course
my hands shook

as I sucked the morphine
and Ativan into the syringe
but my mother

     was on Mt. Fuji,
     ten hours into a two-day hike,
     a borrowed shawl wrapped
     on her black hair.
     I saw the snow
     shake over her purpling feet,
     to the ankles, the shins,

watched it bury,

     bury,

bury her.

NIGHTMARE TRIPTYCH

1.

My mother is alive.

She is driving. She is driving
too fast, trying to tell me everything
from a dozen years
of solitude. She is no older
than I am now: middle-aged
mirrors, twins of a moment,

this moment

when she slams the gas pedal
and we fly off the road.
My mother is dead again.
This time she takes me with her.

2.

In the mirror I am and I am not
my mother. I am alive.

I have so much to teach her, my daughter.
I will drive to her house,

I will drive fast enough for her to see
that we are all dying.

It's just that she's in slow motion.
I'm in real time.

I start the car.

3.

I wake up. She is dead again,
next to me in the mirror.
I am someone I have never been:
an old woman who does not remember
her name. I try to smile.
My face doesn't move,
my mouth stuck open,
an emptiness inside an emptiness.
My mother grins,
shows me all her teeth.

OBSERVER EFFECT

1. Me

The person in the mirror
is made of silver—

she stops the light
moving from my face

and diverts it back
to me, a node

in the ever-branching
multiverse,

a decision point
that makes a world.

Each time I squint,
glasses off, we

bounce the light of
the infinite between us.

2. Her

I watch the silver
one warily, greedily,

like a pigtailed girl
shaking each box under

the Christmas tree, to see if I
can detect my mother inside.

No matter how sly I am—
Oh is that you?

What a surprise to find you here—
I never catch the moment

before the whole experiment
collapses, never glimpse

the place where my mother is
alive and dead,

or neither alive nor dead
but somewhere I don't

have to account for.
Grief is a black box.

I kill her again
when I open it.

10,000 FEET ABOVE SEA LEVEL

A hummingbird hangs like a drone,
tries to sip nectar from my breasts.

My father told me he and my mother,
three marriages ago, camped in this same park,
breathing each other inside the thin sky.

Sometimes you are the flower.

Sometimes you are the elegy yourself.

Sometimes you are the elsewhere,
        the seas, ineluctably rising.

III: UNMENDED

TIMELINE

In Estes Park, Colorado,
a stag flees a wall of fire.

Deep in the interstellar
medium, Voyager 1
leaves us behind.

A man named William Shakespeare
gives his arm to a new vaccine.

Buzzfeed elegizes Los Angeles
next to stills from *Blade Runner 2049*.
You can't tell which is which.

Your brother fails to apologize
to your father, leaves
a truck's worth of garbage
in the basement,
drives away, empty-
handed.

Beirut explodes.

The light
from a star that died
10,000 years ago
discovers your eyes.
You don't notice.

A man with two first names
is murdered in broad daylight

while a girl records it.
No one can breathe.

You don't cry
on Mother's Day.
You cry every day.

Eight billion human beings
stand still.

WE MUST TERRAFORM OURSELVES

In the coffee shop
in the plague
I read a novel set on Mars,

where everything depends
on who owns
the right air.

I smell sanitizer
everywhere,
worry constantly
about my hands.

This antiseptic wind:
a decade ago,
ICU bed, my mother
claws at a blanket.

Hot, she says.

To breathe on Mars
you must
endlessly erode
a scarce resource.

My mother never speaks again.

GHOST STORY WITH NO GHOST IN IT

The low December sun hangs
shadows long as rulers
from each pebble

on the footpath. The lake ice
edges further toward the half-buried
water birds and their boat-bodies.

In my peripheral vision
the smokestack of the mortuary
climbs, stark as an empty flagpole.

I am glad
I can only be unmothered
once. When I held her last,

no mask hid my mouth
from its failure
to save anyone.

CHRISTMAS SEASON

"what happened was [. . .] the gods were us"
—Megan Grumbling, "too many mirrors"

We waited and waited for the snow to come. It did not come. We offered our arms, an army of serums, against an illness so clever we all turned stupid. We dug tornado shelters in the darkest solstice, the farmer's almanac upside down and half on fire as seasons shook out and rearranged their pages. We made cars that drove themselves and steered us straight onto train tracks. We built vacuum-enabled sleeping bags to yank the pressure from the heads of astronauts as they dream, to keep their eyes from bursting. We took stacks of pills and pissed them back into the drinking water, saved it for our gardens. We saved little storm-orphaned dogs and cats, brought them in our homes and dressed them like children, to make up for the way we slaughtered the honeybees. We kissed under mistletoe and dressed the table with poison berries. We praised some god for daring to be born.

PLAGUE / WINTER

We don't talk about the dead.
Already we have forgotten the fires,
the singed animals crawling through ash.

In my neighborhood a murder
of crows claims dominion
over each front yard, jeering

when the dog walkers stride by.
I hear them from my kitchen,
where I try to bake bread

the way my father taught me
without thinking of his fragile bones,
his frequent falls, how easy

to find himself in a hospital
burning with contagion
and then   and then—

Enough.
I still haven't been tested
for what my mother had.

I don't know
how I'm going to die.
I don't want to see it

until I'm already in it,
until I've swum so far
I turn and there is no shore.

WORD / ROOTS

1992 was the first year my family sent me
to college camp, a 12-year-old girl

sleeping nervously in the dorms,
tiptoeing to the showers, praying

for time to fast-forward
so I could do this for real,

skip the terrors of middle school
and dissolve

into monastic study. I learned ancient Greek
because it was the oldest thing

I had heard of, older
than Jesus, an elsewhere.

I learned how to spell my name,
my laurel crown.

*

2020 was not the first but the second year
there were so many hurricanes

we stopped naming them for women
and started naming them for Greek letters,

all the way to iota (ι). They named one
after me, too: *Laura*, Category 4.

She killed 81 people
but that's not what you remember

about 2020, is it? Unless,
of course, it happened to you.

*

My alphabet is built on the back
of this other alphabet, so familiar

yet a little off, like the picture
of my mother at 5 that used to hang

next to the picture of me at 5—
sisters, almost, only one girl

is in black and white,
trapped in the untranslatable past.

A comes from *alpha*,
looks like its daughter:

α   a

Each letter a ghost,
each word a lost world.

*

Now the letters
are stalking us

δ   d   *delta*

o   o   *omicron*

as though language did this:
as though death is outside

our bodies, foreign and ancient,
and not what we carry

on every tongue.

PLAGUE / WINTER

I knit hats
for children,
to keep them
wool-warm,

to keep me
busy. To prove
there is still
one thing

I can do
with unclenched
hands.
Always

in my mind
I used to live
ten years
in the past,

forever propping
my mother's
purpled feet
on the hospital bed.

Now my gaze
spins forward :

      twenty years
      the heat waves

thirty years
the oceans, the storms

forty
the all of it

unmended
unforgiven

The present
skims
my life,
a seafoam.

I trick the dog
into letting me
put a wool sweater
on her shivering

ribs, hurricane
rescue, my own climate
refugee, Cassandra
of the chihuahuas.

The horizon
of days
shrinks
and shrinks

as winter comes
again. Snow
on the sidewalk
since Thanksgiving.

Static everywhere.
Don't slip on it.
Don't breathe it.
Don't go outside.

A YEAR IN THE LATE ANTHROPOCENE

Easter

The dead are unburying themselves
on Everest. As the snow melts, they sit
up, stretch, unbreak femurs, deice cells
of sleeted blood. They survey the shit-
piles, rusted oxygen tanks, snowbound trash
discarded by the lucky and the warm.
They see the mountain excavate the past,
but these glory-drained corpses are not reformed:
They climb. *Because it's there.* They've been here
while the living walked by, reached for the hand
of God, found only the icicle stare
of another ghost. There's no unruined land,
no surface able to withstand our love.
Everything we hide, the dead will crawl above.

Mother's Day

Worlds end before the world ends. Extinction's
another name for sorry-not-sorry.
It's ten red years that my mother's been gone,
and look what she missed: this awful hurry
toward nothing changing. Toward nothing. I save
all the kittens and chihuahuas that I can—
too small to be guilty, none of them brave.
My family of shivering things, clan
of cowards and infertile daughters.

                                    Quit
reading if you're bored of despair. The sun
won't kill us before we off ourselves bit
by burning bit. When I was twenty-one
Al Gore was supposed to save us all.
My mother hadn't yet begun to fall.

All Saints' Day

We salt the earth so we can't haunt ourselves.

I try to recycle. In my backyard,
the squirrels grow fat on old pumpkin shells.
Feeding them is easy—I discard
more than I use, reap more than I sow.
I used to think adults would try, at least,
to save us. Then they died. Now I know
nothing is left between me and the deep
silence of the future. No kings, no gods,
no bees, no water. The moon is better.
The squirrels plan ahead, they calculate odds,
but me, I can't even write: aim for one letter
and my nerve-wracked hand scrawls out another.

Forget the planet.

                I want my mother.

Thanksgiving

We get the food by mail: we don't set foot
outside the house this year. *You'll catch your death,*
my mom would tell us kids, her Rust Belt soot
around the vowels. Which deaths do we accept
as given, as fact? Which ones are plague-stench
murders of neglect? *Hurry, hold your breath,*
we'd say when we passed the graveyard, *unless
you want to catch a ghost.* My burning chest
would give me up, force the spirit through me.
And now I can't call back timbre or tone,
just the mutter of her voice as she
would find the gizzards, unlock flesh from bone.
Thankful is not the word for what we are:
grieving predators hurled around a star.

Advent

I find myself whole in a broken world:
an accident of timing, a good run
in a bad year in a bad decade. Squirreled
away in a calm house with morning sun,
the woman I love and her working lungs
beside me, the plague outside our door
recedes—for just a moment, but oh, one
is enough, more would be greed. There's no floor
to loss, how far it pulls my mind into
the past, the unlivable future: how
will we survive ourselves again, which few
will be spared, what cities fall. But now,
the snow, this street so quiet, to be stuck
exactly where I am: what luck, what luck.

IV: LOVING THE FIRE

BLOOD ON THE MOON & WATER ON MARS

& still my life
seems to matter, to me.
     I can't shake
     the dust off this skeleton,
          give it back
          to the stars
          that birthed it.

Always this impulse
     toward metaphor,
     the selfish need
          to bring the universe
          down to size.

The continents drift
     at the same rate
     our toenails grow.

     I'm a black hole.

          I'm a supernova with human skin.

WAITING FOR A HAIRCUT AT THE END OF THE WORLD

Gas bill twice what it was last year
     It's Russia, they say

Reading a magazine feature : borscht
     good hot or cold

good with meat when you have it
     good with scraps when you don't

Never knew my borscht-eaters
     who fled famine and freeze

in Ukraine to end up
     in Chicago cold as ever

graves I never visited the whole
     decade I lived there

Afraid to look back
     obsessed with looking forward

the sun expanding
     the heat death of the galaxy

Easier than knowing
     what we do to each other

Easier to imagine one wasteland
     forget we live in another :

my brother dead from the hernia
                    waiting to explode

my father's bones soldered
                    with titanium, unbendable

Rigor mortis happens
                    because we need electricity

for our muscles to relax
                    not just to contract

Power does more
                    than clench a fist

Power lets you
                    let go

Behind the stylist's mirror
                    a light flickers, sizzles

It's the wiring, she says
                    tell me if it hurts your eyes

But my eyes always hurt
                    migraines

"cortical spreading depression"
                    electricity misfiring

My doctor wants me to shoot myself
                    in the belly

with the new drug, the one on TV
                because the pills I take

can fuck up my brain
                cause dementia

That's the nightmare
                the spider in your mind

that unknits each neuron
                from its sisters

my mother so broken
                she could not speak

last word she said
                dying not yet dying

wires   tubes   monitors
                blanket up to chin

hot, she said so I
                took the blanket

off
                hot

My stylist puts her beautiful
                hands on me

asks what I want
                off

I say

take it all off

INJECTION DAY

Your burning body

the bruise inked on your belly

the infusion spreading through the layers of you—

        the skin pearlescent, almost see-through

        the subcutaneous fat gathered to protect you

        the muscles under strain from the constant ache

        the bones that hold you as you walk through this world

        the joints eaten by the mystery of your illness—

you ask me to hold the needle

steady your shaking hand

        and I am disastrous

        I make it worse

        I cannot feel what you feel

and still you forgive me

as we praise this moment

as we love the fire

in its subsiding

DUPLEX FOR ISAAC

We were sixteen. I adored you so much,
I lost my voice talking to you that night.

        When I lost my voice, talking near you that night,
        your mother brought me honeyed tea.

Who brought your mother bitter honey, sweet tea,
when she sat shiva, all the mirrors sheeted?

        She sat, silent, sheeted the mirrors,
        your body already gone. I missed the funeral,

missed your beauty, already beyond
what I knew. We weren't even thirty.

        What did I know, not even thirty?
        In my head, you are that midnight boy forever, untouchable,

untouched. Oh my midnight head, my dead friend.
We were sixteen. I didn't adore you enough.

THIS REGULARLY HAPPENS

During the lockdown drill I forget to wait
        for the code word that means ALL CLEAR

is real and not part of the disaster,
        an easy trick learned by everyone

who grew up with active shooter drills,
        which is to say: everyone younger than me.

I let the students start talking again,
        their nervous energy visible

like motion lines in the manga
        my white friends read in high school

and then the loudspeaker speaks
        the code I'd forgotten. The students stop

dead, look at me with unsimulated fear:
        I had made a mistake.

Twenty years ago I was in college, waiting
        for CNN's video to buffer

because the whole world
        was watching the Columbine kids

climb out their windows, drop God
        knows how far to the ground.

I still can't breathe
      when I remember the arm

in the window frame
      letting go of the arm dangling below.

Thirty years ago my mother quit teaching
      when a boy punched her in the face.

She tried to break up a fight,
      became the fight instead.

She walked out
      and never walked in again.

I look back in my students' faces,
      their freckled worries fighting

their impossible youth,
      say something like, *Good, that was the real*

ALL CLEAR, if this weren't a drill . . .
      and try not to show in my body

what I see in my mind:
      their bodies, the gun,

my foolish hand
      still opening the door.

SIX YEARS AFTER *OBERGEFELL*, MY COWORKER ASKS ME IF MY MARRIAGE IS LEGAL IN THE STATE OF COLORADO

and I hide my shock gracelessly,
grateful for once for the mask
keeping our breaths in our own faces.
How much each of us is permitted
to not know: what we are lucky to never
learn. My students, bless them,
think *queerbaiting* is something a TV show does
and not something a group of men does
when they want to hurt what they fear.
They go to school mass and hear
that God loves them. No one points
to a verse and spits, no rocks are thrown.
They trust that the world owes them middle age
because, after all, here I am,
boring in my dailiness.
We occupy a different country:
these teenagers in their reckless beauty
thinking justice is so obvious,
so clearly correct, that it is already historical—
and this woman (individually, achingly kind),
walking through a world where I am so new
as to be unthinkable, futuristic.
I tell her about the law of the land
and she congratulates me—for the Supreme Court,
I think, though that Court is dead
and this one has its fist in my gut—
and I am too tired to say I am glad
that this time around the court came first
and the plague came after, that when
we looked at each other in fear and said,

One of us could die from this,
there was a solution to the problem
of hospital visits, of the house,
of the breathing machines.
What luck I have, allowed to remember
the terror that I was not forced
to live.

SAFE WORDS

The world is hostage to our ancestors,
        their foolish pleasures,
                their fossil harvests—

and I am fettered by my petty griefs,
        tiny, inevitable, but it feels
                like a galaxy of loss—

the dead stacked like wood
        behind us, the future dead
                waiting for the axe—

billions of humans overlaid
        like transparencies in a biology textbook,
                flip and strip the skeleton bare—

but still when she touches my neck
        with her mouth I am shivered
                by desire

to live, to make something
        with my body, to keep my blood
                inside my impossible skin

and believe the world
        will not end until we tell it
                exactly when to stop—

HOME MAINTENANCE

1.

You stalk the roof in your winter gear,
clearing gutters, blowing leaves, crawling
to see the shingles that keep the rain out,
when it rains. Yesterday your father scoffed,
Water's not going anywhere, and we laughed
and laughed. You can see the future:
the hoses run dry, the grass dead all over,
our rain barrels a new currency.
You stash seeds in the deep freezer, machetes
in the garage by the bikes we barely ride
but hang on to, just in case. This is how
we live now: *just in case.*

2.

In case the fires.

          In case the neighbors.

In case the Court.

          In case the hospitals.

In case Texas.

          In case the President.

In case the oceans.

          In case the ice caps.

In case God.

          In case no God.

In case my brain.

          In case your body.

In case me first.

          In case you first.

3.

I help you down from the roof—
    I'm too afraid to go up the ladder

so you do what needs to be done,
    you walk where I can't make myself go.

IF THIS IS ALL A SIMULATION

and we are the NPCs
in some vicious game

I am grateful

      that I am not a solo traveler
          glowing idly
               in the outer realms
          waiting to be activated
               by some stranger's need

      that I have you
          as my companion

      that in all this scriptedness
          our lines
               have yet to repeat

      that the program
          generated this little house
               cats   dogs
          the flush of your skin
               the hot whiskey
          of your voice
               my name inside it

IF THE SUN EXPLODES WE WILL NOT KNOW FOR EIGHT MINUTES

Pine resin oozes from the scars
of carved names, love an accidental archaeology.

Across the campground, a marching band
counts off in martial time, rehearses glory.

Swallows rollercoaster around power lines.

A mule deer fawn leapfrogs into view,
sees you, and unappears.

MIDLIFE NEBULA

In that otherwhere, stars
glue themselves together

out of dust. Thus
the unmarriageable specks

gain names, which are gifts
we grant to those wells of gravity

we deign to notice.
Yet the whole gleaming fabric

is a sham, a weave of dark
and ungodly matter warping

together the lights that appear
apart. We cling so fiercely

to the evidence of sparks:
proof that someone loves us,

they say, that someone wanted
all of us to happen. But

what's visible is accident:
the collision of

two drifting, dreamless
bodies, such dumb luck

mistaken for design.

POEM IN WHICH I FAIL TO TEACH HOMER

When Sally Ride suited up for America, the NASA engineers asked her if 100 tampons was the correct number for one 32-year-old woman to spend one week in space. *That is not the correct number*, she said. I tell this to my students because they are teenage girls and they already know the world thinks they are a mystery. We know more about the surface of Jupiter. The engineers counted everything, limited even the souvenirs each astronaut could take because, pound for pound, fuel was so precious. How many gallons of menstrual blood did they calculate for? What horror as they imagined a female body escaping the Earth? In class we are talking about Penelope, how she fooled the suitors for three years because they knew nothing of weaving, of women's work. *Didn't they get suspicious?* one girl asks. *Once I told my dad I had PMS for six weeks straight and he believed me*, replies another. *Men don't know anything.* They hate Odysseus, these girls, they have him pegged as the villain. When I was in school they wheeled an ancient television into our classroom one day, spent eternities hooking every plug to every socket, and then we watched seven people die, live on TV. Sally Ride was scheduled for the next mission. She never flew again. My students don't know about the Challenger explosion, they are living through different disasters. They are angrier than I knew how to be at 15. *Why does it matter if Penelope is faithful when Odysseus sleeps with every woman he meets?* they ask. I tell them it doesn't matter to us but it matters to Ithaca. Ithaca isn't fair. When Odysseus, salt-crusted and naked, flirts with Nausicaa, so young that she still plays catch, my girls talk about the grown men who follow them, the men who call after them, the men who scare them. *I'm sorry this happens to you*, I say, *it happened to me too.* Earth isn't fair. Sally Ride knew the Challenger inside and out. She lived in that ship, further at sea than Odysseus could dream of. In the press conference before launch, they asked, *Do you ever cry on the job?* When Penelope weeps, Homer says her mind moves elsewhere. No one knows what she knows.

V: POEMS FROM HAVEN

"And God blessed them, and God said unto them, Be fruitful, and multiply, and replenish the earth, and subdue it: and have dominion over the fish of the sea, and over the fowl of the air, and over every living thing that moveth upon the earth."

—Genesis 1:28

BLUE PLANET

When the aliens we all believe in
come to study our wreckage,

they will find only our bleary
agonies: plastic islands carved

of trash, plague graves, corroded
plaques for the planetful

of species we took down with us.
Nothing will explain our madness

was not mere murder:
we had solved so much.

We were too many.
We could not stop

giving the world
what we thought it wanted:

us.

DOMINION

When the waters turned brown
we shot our gaze skyward.
The birds took no pity.

We'd come down from the trees,
after all, to ruin what we touched.
There was only one

direction left to devour.
We built ourselves wings,
called the first ship *Dominion*,

gloated as we rose above feathered things.
In the onboard lab, the caged parrot
learned to speak as the captain:

preening her cloak, she spat orders
that no one followed, cursed the boy
who shrank as he fed her.

Fifty years old, the last of her kind captured
and not bred, she plumed her voice
to breaking, answered only to "Master."

THE CARTOGRAPHER

If I had my way, every ship
        would be named *Orpheus*,
because I cannot stop singing
        for what I abandoned.

It was blue and living in the old
        moonshot photos—
I've seen whole films
        with names like *Blue Planet*

and *The Life of Birds*.
        The children mock me
when I reread the maps
        of continents I never touched.

But I hear the lyre work
        beneath the names—
Tanzania, Uruguay, Canada—
        the syllables call to me

Turn your gaze, the words
        like an echo in the mouth
of a creature I saw
        in the documentary

my mother played to keep me still:
        the superb lyrebird,
whose mimic throat could recreate
        anything,

even the whir of the camera
        as it captured
the song, the animal unaware
        of what it uttered.

NOW THEY ARE DEAD AND I WEIGH NOTHING

When I sleep
in my vertical
plastic coffin,
I dream

I am an Earthling
again, lying
about the number
on the scale,

my first sin
spent in the school
nurse's office,
those annual

humiliations:
height
weight
spine

Those other girls,
their slim
limbs,
their long braids,

their fox faces
sharp against
my roundness,
my taking up space

INERTIAL FORCE CREATES SUSTAINED NORMAL FORCE

We mistake the pull between us
      for gravity—it feels so like

home, as though you
      are the planet

and I am the sky, or I
      the lunar body and you

the tides. Your hand is heavy
      on my spine, a force

that can't be faked.
      With you I can

ignore the liquid spin
      of stars

through portholes,
      the way

rotation glues us
      to the ground—this illusion

that we still feel
      an up, a down.

THE MEDIC

When I break open a body,
      I part atoms

that were birthed
      in a supernova,

flung into the black,
      and regathered

into this elaboration
      of tubes.

Everything comes
      from something else,

so why grieve
      what we chose

to destroy? I can't heal
      what I can't cut.

No maggots left
      to eat dead flesh.

I named my blade
      Survival.

EVERY OBJECT ITS OWN ELEGY

We burn the dead
and bury them in our bodies

as phosphorus, nitrogen, carbon
saved in the soil

and resurrected as food.
Therefore: I do not mourn.

Therefore: none are gone
until all are gone.

This is how we know
that we are better than

our ancestors and their starving
Earth. When you kill,

you must eat
what you kill,

lest it kill you
with its absence.

ARK

We needed to pretend it was destiny—
abandoning the world that made us.

Two by two we catalogued the DNA,
built an archive to float

above every living thing we gave up on
(everything that was not ourselves).

The Pope herself blessed our endeavor,
laid hands on the launchpad,

the seed storage, the fetal pigs
in cold stasis. God is merciful

because He lets His disciples
escape the disasters they make.

When we reached the surface,
the zoologists brought the captain

a dove, an olive branch
bioprinted for the occasion.

IT COULD SAVE US

The neighborhood looks safe,
how we used to mean it:
the picket fence, the weeping
willow, the windows of genteel glass.

We made a replica of the world we killed
and we named it Haven,
as though it could save us.
Every object its own elegy.

The willow's grotesque roots grope
the oxygen dome's edge.
The membrane pulses,
a frontier.

The more we breathe,
the closer we are
to what will starve us:
the itch for freedom, for unearthly air.

NONE ARE GONE UNTIL ALL ARE GONE

I refuse

to mourn the old
world. For this

I am called strange.
No one asks

my daughter to weep
for the starry cauldron

she wears as flesh,
to pledge allegiance

to Theia,
the antique planet

that smashed apart
the molten Earth

to make the moon
we once walked on.

Every surface is carved
from something that died

to create it.

VI: WE RUIN EVERYTHING

WE THE DESTROYERS

And what if the world isn't ending?

I know about the others
who were certain they lived in the twilight;

they made ceremonies, shaved
their bodies, killed themselves

before they could be crushed
by time. Holy fools who

mistook their feelings for history.
They knew what the earth deserves

from us: our absence.
What if it just goes on this way,

ugly, terrifying, so that I forget
the texture of crumbling flyleaf

in the rotting book from my library,
so that no one is old enough to remember

what it felt like to solve a problem,
to really fix it—no more smallpox,

not anywhere, we did that, we
the destroyers did that.

In the version where I am wrong,
we keep going. We ruin everything

and salt the wounds and still
something green and bloody comes back.

We are not the hard, unforgiving seeds
but the fire that cleaves them open.

ACKNOWLEDGMENTS & NOTES

Versions of these poems appeared in the following publications, sometimes in earlier forms:

Boulevard: "We the Destroyers"
Cotton Xenomorph: "Poem in Which I Fail to Teach Homer"
The Dodge: "Wing-Deep in Gin and Tonic"
Limp Wrist: "Poem in Which I Fail to Teach Homer" (reprint), "Six Years After *Obergefell*, My Coworker Asks Me If My Marriage Is Legal in the State of Colorado"
Moist Poetry Journal: "10,000 Feet Above Sea Level," "If the Sun Explodes We Will Not Know for Eight Minutes"
Paperbark: "Solstice or Something"
Public School Poetry: "Dementia / Elsewhere," "Ekphrasis on an Out-of-Focus Photo Scanned by My Aunt," "You, Meg Murry"
Rise Up Review: "To Outweigh"
Rust and Moth: "Blood on the Moon & Water on Mars"
SWWIM Every Day: "Grief Counseling in the Late Anthropocene"
Watershed Review: "Escaping / Air," "Tell Me, What Else Should I Have Done?," "Water / Pollution"
West Trade Review: "For Mary Ann, Fifteen Years Too Late"

"Grief Counseling in the Late Anthropocene": The "Anthropocene" is a proposed (but unofficial) epoch of geologic time, meant to designate the period when human activity has made a major, detectable impact on planetary systems.

"Tell Me, What Else Should I Have Done?" is a response to Mary Oliver's poem "The Summer Day."

"On Lake Erie with My Brother's Ghost" takes its first line from Joannie Stangeland's poem "Things I Forgot about Love."

"Cold Abecedarian Ending with a Line from Emily Dickinson" takes its final line from Dickinson's poem "A narrow Fellow in the Grass."

"Arctic heat record is like Mediterranean, says UN": The title of this poem was a BBC News headline on December 14, 2021.

"Wing-Deep in Gin and Tonic" is for Cathy Muskett, who inspired the title.

"You, Meg Murry": In addition to Madeleine L'Engle's classic novel *A Wrinkle in Time*, the title of this poem nods to Archibald MacLeish's poem "You, Andrew Marvell."

"Observer Effect" refers, imprecisely, to the concept in physics that the act of observing a phenomenon alters the state of that phenomenon; this concept is often illustrated through the famous thought experiment known as Schrödinger's Cat.

"We Must Terraform Ourselves" is inspired by Kim Stanley Robinson's classic Mars Trilogy, specifically *Red Mars*. "Terraforming" refers to the hypothetical alteration of a planet's atmosphere and environment to make it more Earthlike and habitable to humans.

"Duplex for Isaac" is for Isaac Meyers.

"This Regularly Happens": After most mass shootings in the United States, the satirical newspaper *The Onion* runs an identical article (with only the byline changed), titled "'No Way to Prevent This,' Says Only Nation Where This Regularly Happens."

"Six Years After *Obergefell*, My Coworker Asks Me If My Marriage Is Legal in the State of Colorado": The US Supreme Court case *Obergefell v. Hodges* affirmed the constitutionality of same-sex marriage in 2015.

"If This Is All a Simulation": In gaming, "NPC" stands for "nonplayer character." An NPC is a character who is not the protagonist or in any way controlled by the gamer—a kind of extra to make the world seem more real or to further the plot. Some philosophers have suggested that the world as we perceive it is actually a massive simulation and that we are constructs populating that simulation.

Many of the poems in this book, especially in section V, are inspired by the work of the naturalist and broadcaster Sir David Attenborough.

THANKS

Thank you for guidance, support, and friendship to Courtney LeBlanc and Riot in Your Throat. I am so honored to be a part of this amazing press. Your commitment to feminist poetry is a gift to our difficult world.

Thank you to Gwendal Cottin for the excellent cover art, Shanna Compton for the interior book design, and Kirsten Birst for the cover design. Thank you to Bianca Dagostino for your work as the Riot in Your Throat intern—your work is invaluable!

Thank you to the readers and editors of the journals where many of these poems were previously published.

Thank you to Brittney Corrigan, Carolina Hotchandani, and Claire Wahmanholm for your kindness and generosity in reading and blurbing this book.

This book is dedicated to my friend and fellow poet Laura Paul Watson, who provided valuable feedback, insight, and encouragement during what turned out to be the last year of her life. Laura was a beautiful person, a thoughtful friend, and a brilliant writer. If you are reading this book, please seek out and read Laura Paul Watson's amazing poetry: "Because other and still other / Lauras flow, I am and I am not Laura."

This book is also in memory of my stepbrother, Peter Heinze. I miss you, Pete.

This book would not exist without the support and encouragement of family members, friends, teachers, and other loved ones. I am especially grateful to Kasey Evans and Melissa Fite Johnson for early feedback on this book as a whole; I couldn't have finished it without you! Several of these poems germinated in a workshop taught by Carolyn Forché at the Lighthouse Writers Workshop in Denver, and I am grateful both to Carolyn and to my classmates for the inspiration. My eternal love and gratitude go to my local writing group here in Denver: Myntha Anthym, Kate Madrid, Aurora Passin, and Vinitia Swonger.

Every December, I run a challenge with a group of poets to write a poem a day. This group has become a lifeline for me and a deep wellspring of creativity. This book simply would not exist without this group. I am grateful for each one of you: your creativity, your words, and your trust. This is an incomplete list, but special thanks go to our regular crew who have shown up for years and years: Aurora, Brian, Brittney, Carolina, Catie, Courtney, Ellen, Emily, Joannie, Kate, Katie, Lisa, Liz, Matt, Melissa, Teo, Vinitia, Wally. This is certainly not everyone! Anyone who has been part of this group has had a hand in this book, and I am grateful.

Thank you to my family, especially Richard Heinze, Thomas Passin, and James Passin.

Thank you to my students and colleagues at St. Mary's Academy and elsewhere. You are in this book.

For a whole wonderful, joyous, poetry-filled life, thank you to Aurora Passin, who makes the impossible possible. You are a poem.

ABOUT THE AUTHOR

Laura Passin is the author of *Borrowing Your Body* (Riot in Your Throat) and *All Sex and No Story* (Rabbit Catastrophe Press). Laura earned her PhD in English Literature at Northwestern and her MFA in Creative Writing at the University of Oregon. Her writing has appeared in a wide range of publications, including *Prairie Schooner, Glass: A Journal of Poetry, The Toast, Electric Literature*, and *Best New Poets*. Her work has been nominated for the Pushcart prize and *Best of the Net* anthology. Laura lives in Denver with too many pets.

ABOUT THE PRESS

Riot in Your Throat is an independent press that
publishes fierce, feminist poetry.

Support independent authors, artists, and presses.

Visit us online:
www.riotinyourthroat.com

RIOT IN YOUR THROAT BOOKS

Sarah Beddow   *Dispatches from Frontier Schools*
Kathryn Bratt-Pfotenhauer   *Bad Animal*
Kimberly Casey   *Where the Water Begins*
Sonia Greenfield   *All Possible Histories*
Brett Elizabeth Jenkins   *Brilliant Little Body*
Melissa Fite Johnson   *Green*
Melissa Fite Johnson   *Midlife Abecedarian*
Hadley Jones   *Devout*
Hilary King   *Stitched on Me*
Frances Klein   *Another Life*
Courtney LeBlanc   *Exquisite Bloody, Beating Heart*
Courtney LeBlanc   *Her Dark Everything*
Jill Michelle   *Underwater*
Shilo Niziolek   *Little Deaths*
Laura Passin   *Borrowing Your Body*
Laura Passin   *We the Destroyers*
Sara Quinn Rivara   *Little Beast*
Laurie Rachkus Uttich   *Somewhere, a Woman
Lowers the Hem of Her Skirt*
Karen J. Weyant   *Avoiding the Rapture*